The Wizard of Oz

Wise Publications
part of The Music Sales Group

London/New York/Paris/Sydney/Copenhagen/Berlin/Madrid/Hong Kong/Tokyo

Published by
Wise Publications
14-15 Berners Street,
London W1T 3LJ, UK.

Exclusive Distributors:
Music Sales Limited
Distribution Centre, Newmarket Road,
Bury St Edmunds, Suffolk IP33 3YB, UK.
Music Sales Corporation
180 Madison Avenue, 24th Floor,
New York NY 10016, USA.
Music Sales Pty Limited
Units 3-4, 17 Willfox Street, Condell Park
NSW 2200, Australia.

Order No. AM1010075
ISBN 978-1-78305-843-3

This book © Copyright 2015 Wise Publications,
a division of Music Sales Limited.

Unauthorised reproduction of any part of this
publication by any means including photocopying is an
infringement of copyright.

Edited by Adrian Hopkins
Music processed by shedwork.com
Photographs courtesy of Authenticated News/Archive Photos/Getty Images

Printed in the EU

Your Guarantee of Quality
As publishers, we strive to produce every book to the
highest commercial standards.
This book has been carefully designed to minimise awkward
page turns and to make playing from it a real pleasure.
Particular care has been given to specifying acid-free, neutral-sized paper
made from pulps which have not been elemental chlorine bleached.
This pulp is from farmed sustainable forests and was
produced with special regard for the environment.
Throughout, the printing and binding have been planned to
ensure a sturdy, attractive publication which should give years of enjoyment.
If your copy fails to meet our high standards,
please inform us and we will gladly replace it.

www.musicsales.com

Contents

Tuning your ukulele

The ukulele is unusual among string instruments in that the strings are not tuned in order of pitch.

Here are the tuning notes for a ukulele on a piano keyboard.

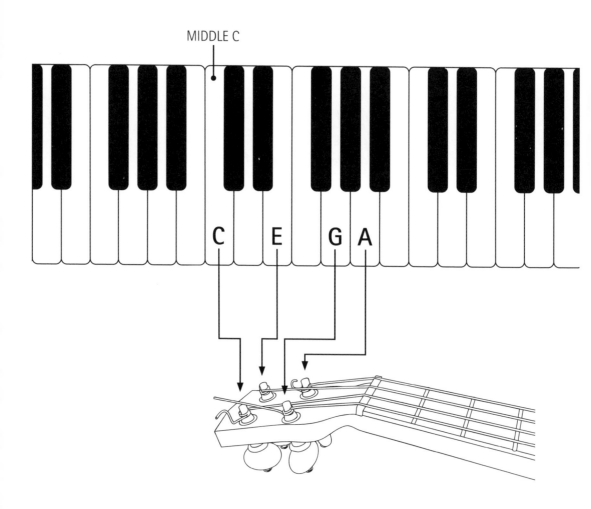

A good way to remember the notes of the strings is this little tune:

Reading chord boxes

Chord diagrams are shown with the nut uppermost. In a standard diagram, the thick horizontal line at the top of the diagram represents the nut, while the large dots show the finger positions.

The other horizontal lines are the frets, while the vertical lines represent the strings. If a string is played open, this is shown by an 'o' above the string. If a string is not played, this is shown by an 'x'.

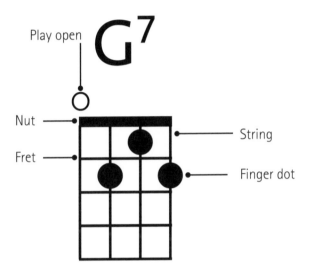

A barre chord is indicated by a curved line across the relevant strings at the barred fret.

For chords played higher up the neck, the lowest fret is indicated at the top of the diagram.

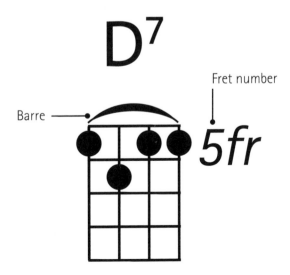

*T*his classic 1939 MGM musical fantasy brought together Judy Garland, some spectacular sets and a selection of very memorable songs in an elaborate production that has since become one of the most famous films ever made.

Success was by no means assured at the time. Seventeen-year-old Judy Garland was a little too old for her role as the little Kansas farm girl Dorothy Gale, but she made the part her own anyway. MGM barely made its money back with the initial release, although the film went on to earn many millions in later years. The songs, though, by 'Yip' Harburg and Harold Arlen, sounded like winners from the start.

'Over The Rainbow' is sung by Dorothy some 6 minutes into the film. She has been having a bad day with a crabby neighbour but gets short shrift from her busy Aunt Em who briskly tells her to find a place 'where she won't get into any trouble'. The song, offered as a young girl's reverie about whether such an impossibly ideal place might actually exist, won an Academy Award and acquired unexpected resonances over the years.

The film's second song comes after a twister has hit the farm house and a window sash has hit Dorothy in the head, propelling her from the sepia Mid-West into Technicolor-drenched Munchkinland. Here her guide is Glinda, the Good Witch of the North, who coaxes the pint-sized Munchkins from their hiding places ('Come Out, Come Out, Wherever You Are') and reveals that the falling Kansas farm house has miraculously killed the Wicked Witch of the East, so making Dorothy an instant heroine. Dorothy protests ('It Really Was No Miracle') but celebrations ensue with 'Ding Dong The Witch Is Dead'. A welcoming medley from various Munchkin delegations follow: 'Lullaby League', 'Lollipop Guild', and 'We Welcome You To Munchkinland'. It is then revealed that a Wicked Witch of the West also exists ('worse than her dead sister') posing a new threat to Dorothy's safety. Protected by a pair of magic ruby slippers, Dorothy is tunefully advised to 'Follow The Yellow Brick Road' and informed 'You're Off To See The Wizard' as the Munchkins send her on her way to the distant Emerald City, where resides the fabled Wizard of Oz who may be able to help her to get back to Kansas.

Most of the remaining songs are there mainly to help move the plot along, the exceptions being the much-loved 'If I Only Had A Brain', 'If I Only Had A Heart' and 'If I Only Had The Nerve' — shortfalls musically lamented by three eccentric companions Dorothy meets on her journey, respectively the Scarecrow, the Tin Man and the Cowardly Lion.

When the trio emerges from a forbidding forest, they hear the disembodied 'Optimistic Voices (You're Out Of The Woods)' and on eventually reaching the Emerald City, they are treated to a rousingly patriotic number ('The Merry Old Land Of Oz') by its citizens. At barely one hour into the film and with 40 minutes still to go comes the final song, the now-emboldened Cowardly Lion's 'If I Were King Of The Forest'.

For the final reel Herbert Stothart's Academy Award-winning score artfully revisits the melodies of several songs already heard. There is a brief instrumental reprise of 'Over The Rainbow' when Dorothy finally awakes from her delirious dream to find herself back in sepia-tinted Kansas surrounded by the familiar faces of family and friends; faces that had been transplanted to some of the characters in her fantasy. The film ends with Dorothy's tremulous voice and Stothart's swooping score reminding us simply that 'There's no place like home'.

Come Out, Come Out, Wherever You Are/
It Really Was No Miracle

Words by E.Y. Harburg
Music by Harold Arlen

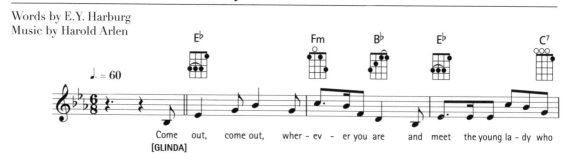

Come out, come out, wher-ev-er you are and meet the young la-dy who
[GLINDA]

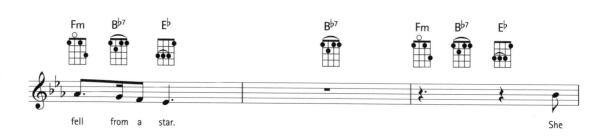

fell from a star.

She

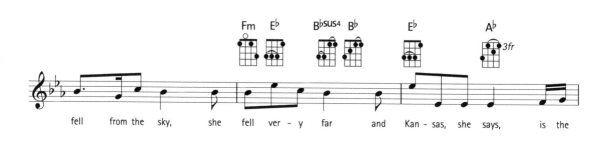

fell from the sky, she fell ver-y far and Kan-sas, she says, is the

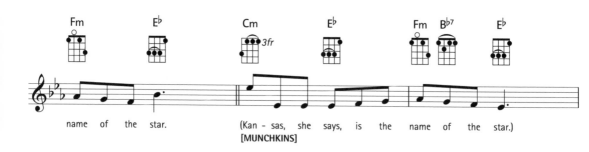

name of the star. (Kan-sas, she says, is the name of the star.)
[MUNCHKINS]

© Copyright 1939 Feist Leo Incorporated.
EMI United Partnership Limited.
All Rights Reserved. International Copyright Secured.

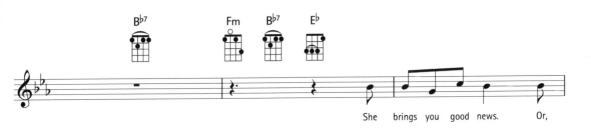

She brings you good news. Or,

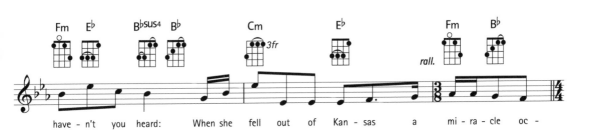

have-n't you heard: When she fell out of Kan-sas a mi-ra-cle oc-

♩ = 130

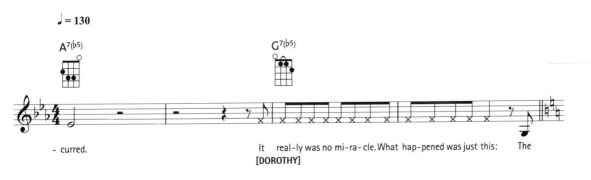

- curred. It real-ly was no mi-ra-cle. What hap-pened was just this: The
[DOROTHY]

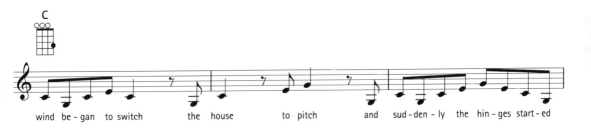

wind be-gan to switch the house to pitch and sud-den-ly the hin-ges start-ed

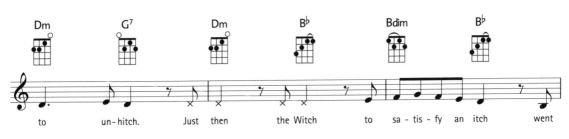

to un-hitch. Just then the Witch to sa-tis-fy an itch went

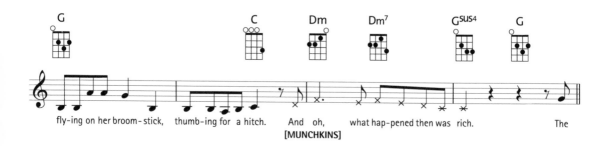

fly-ing on her broom-stick, thumb-ing for a hitch. And oh, what hap-pened then was rich. The

[MUNCHKINS]

house be-gan to pitch, the kit-chen took a slitch. It land-ed on the Wick-ed Witch in the

mid-dle of a ditch, which_____ was not a health-y si - tu-a-tion for the Wick-ed

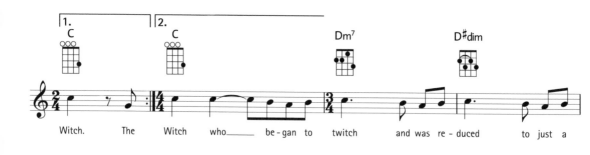

Witch. The Witch who_____ be-gan to twitch and was re-duced to just a

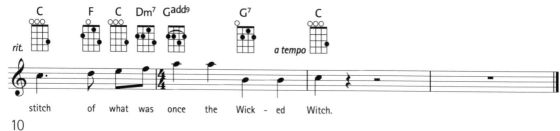

stitch of what was once the Wick - ed Witch.

10

Lullaby League/Lollipop Guild/
We Welcome You To Munchkinland

Words by E.Y. Harburg
Music by Harold Arlen

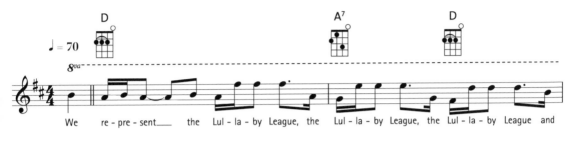

We re-pre-sent___ the Lul-la-by League, the Lul-la-by League, the Lul-la-by League and

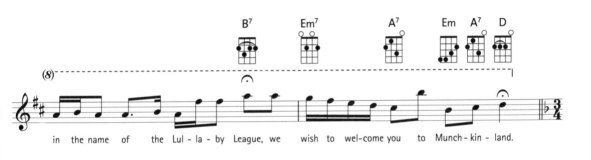

in the name of the Lul-la-by League, we wish to wel-come you to Munch-kin-land.

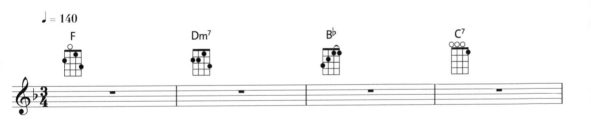

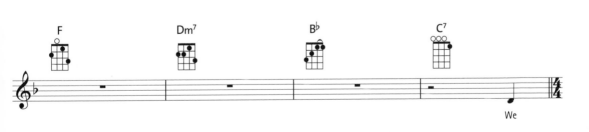

We

© Copyright 1939 Feist Leo Incorporated.
EMI United Partnership Limited.
All Rights Reserved. International Copyright Secured.

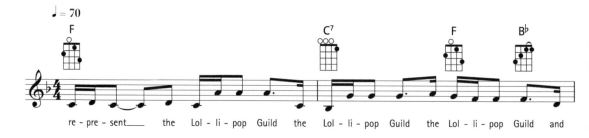

re - pre - sent____ the Lol - li - pop Guild the Lol - li - pop Guild the Lol - li - pop Guild and

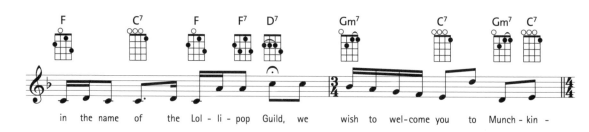

in the name of the Lol - li - pop Guild, we wish to wel-come you to Munch - kin -

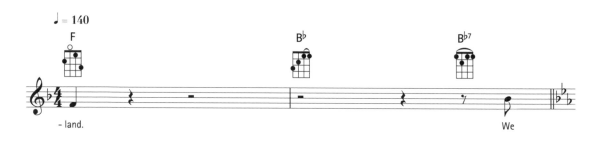

- land. We

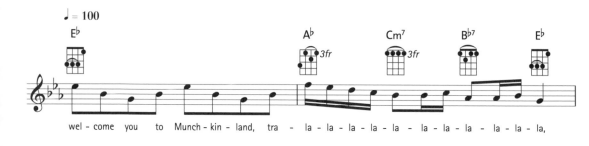

wel - come you to Munch - kin - land, tra - la - la - la - la - la - la - la - la - la - la - la - la,

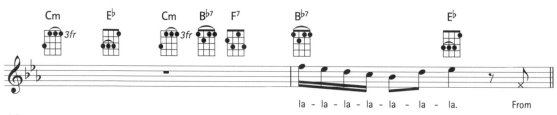

la - la - la - la - la - la - la. From

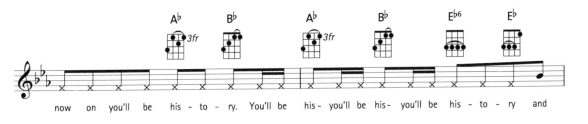

now on you'll be his-to-ry. You'll be his- you'll be his- you'll be his-to-ry and

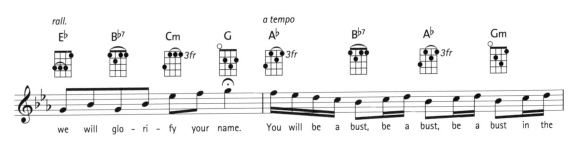

we will glo-ri-fy your name. You will be a bust, be a bust, be a bust in the

hall of fame! La - la - la - la - la - la - la - la - la - la - la - la,

la - la - la - la - la - la - la. La - la - la - la - la - la - la - la - la - la - la,

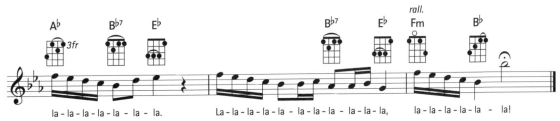

la-la-la-la-la-la-la. La-la-la-la-la-la-la-la-la-la-la, la-la-la-la-la-la!

Over The Rainbow

Words by E.Y. Harburg
Music by Harold Arlen

Some - where   o - ver the rain - bow   way   up   high,

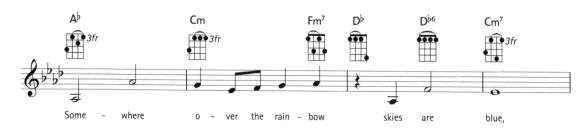

there's   a   land   that   I   heard   of   once   in   a   lul - la - by.

Some - where   o - ver the rain - bow   skies   are   blue,

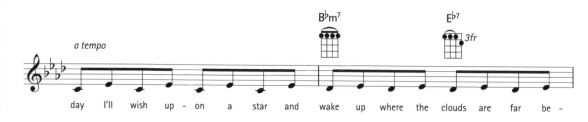

and   the   dreams that you dare   to   dream real - ly do come   true.   Some

day   I'll   wish   up - on   a   star   and   wake   up   where   the   clouds   are   far   be -

© Copyright 1938 EMI Feist Catalog Incorporated.
EMI United Partnership Limited.
All Rights Reserved. International Copyright Secured.

Ding Dong The Witch Is Dead

Words by E.Y. Harburg
Music by Harold Arlen

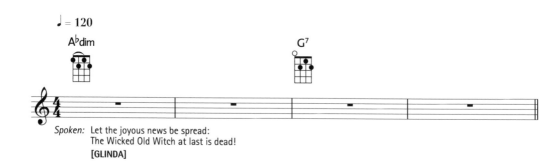

Spoken: Let the joyous news be spread:
The Wicked Old Witch at last is dead!
[GLINDA]

Ding   dong! The Witch is dead.   Which old Witch? The Wick-ed Witch!   Ding   dong! The Wick-ed Witch is
[MUNCHKINS]

dead.   Wake   up, you sleep-y head,   rub your eyes, get out of bed.   Wake   up, the Wick-ed Witch is

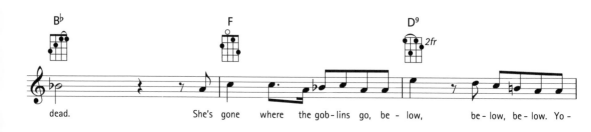

dead.   She's   gone   where   the gob-lins go, be - low,   be - low, be - low. Yo -

© Copyright 1939 Feist Leo Incorporated.
EMI United Partnership Limited.
All Rights Reserved. International Copyright Secured.

-ho,   let's o - pen up and   sing   and ring the bells out. Ding   dong,   the mer - ry - oh,

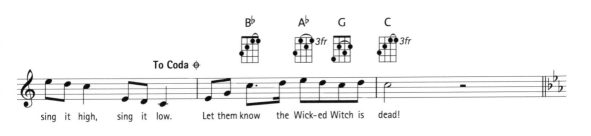

To Coda ⊕

sing it high,   sing it low.   Let them know   the Wick-ed Witch is   dead!

(Instrumental)

molto rall.

As

[MAYOR]

17

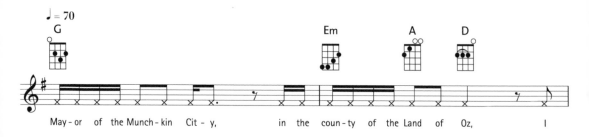

♩ = 70

May - or of the Munch - kin Cit - y, in the coun - ty of the Land of Oz, I

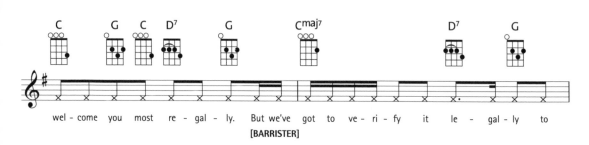

wel - come you most re - gal - ly. But we've got to ve - ri - fy it le - gal - ly to

[BARRISTER]

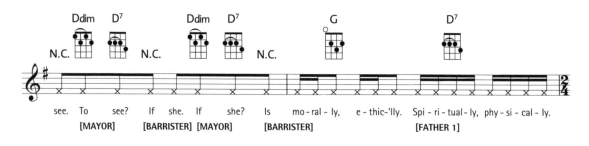

see. To see? If she. If she? Is mo - ral - ly, e - thic - 'lly. Spi - ri - tual - ly, phy - si - cal - ly.

[MAYOR] [BARRISTER] [MAYOR] [BARRISTER] [FATHER 1]

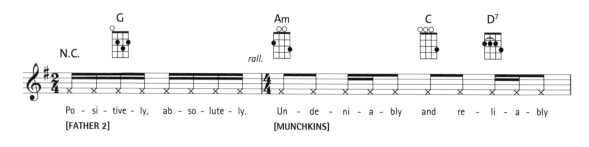

Po - si - tive - ly, ab - so - lute - ly. Un - de - ni - a - bly and re - li - a - bly

[FATHER 2] [MUNCHKINS]

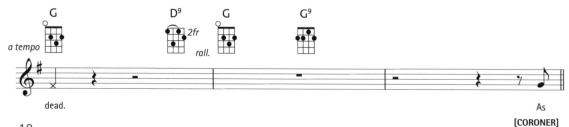

a tempo

rall.

dead.

As

[CORONER]

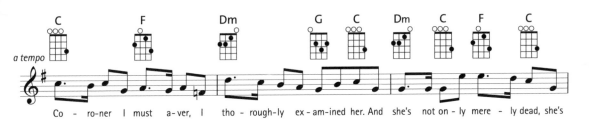

Co - ro-ner I must a-ver, I tho - rough-ly ex - am-ined her. And she's not on - ly mere - ly dead, she's

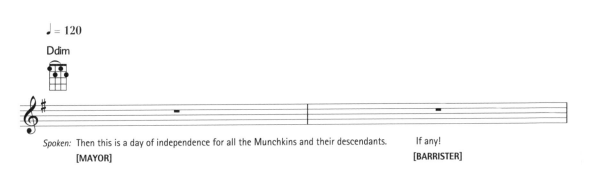

accel.

real - ly most sin - cere - ly dead.

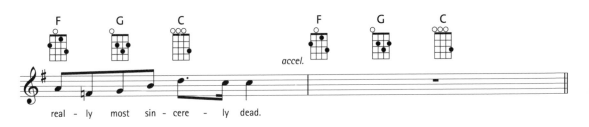

♩ = 120

Ddim

Spoken: Then this is a day of independence for all the Munchkins and their descendants. If any!

[MAYOR] [BARRISTER]

D♭dim

D.S. al Coda

Yes, let the joyous news be spread: The Wicked Old Witch at last is dead!

[MAYOR]

Coda

Let them know the Wick - ed Witch is dead!

Follow The Yellow Brick Road/
We're Off To See The Wizard

Words by E.Y. Harburg
Music by Harold Arlen

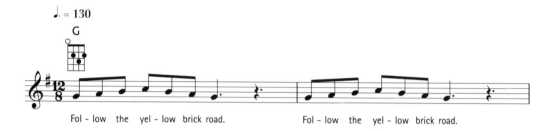

Fol - low the yel - low brick road. Fol - low the yel - low brick road.

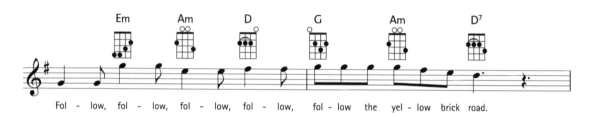

Fol - low, fol - low, fol - low, fol - low, fol - low the yel - low brick road.

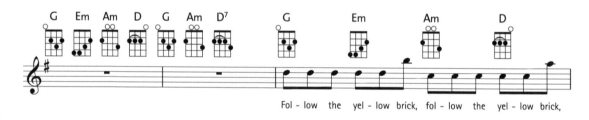

Fol - low the yel - low brick, fol - low the yel - low brick,

fol - low the yel - low brick road. You're

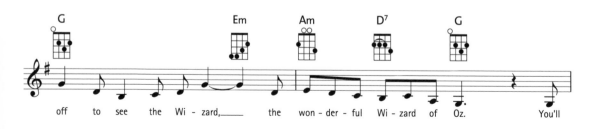

off to see the Wi - zard, the won - der - ful Wi - zard of Oz. You'll

© Copyright 1939 EMI Feist Catalog Incorporated.
EMI United Partnership Limited.
All Rights Reserved. International Copyright Secured.

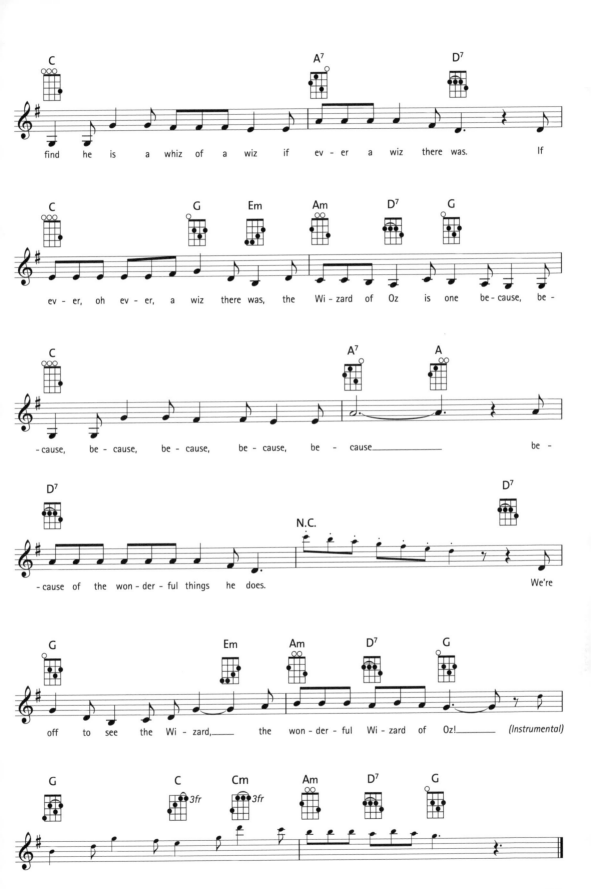

If I Only Had A Brain

Words by E.Y. Harburg
Music by Harold Arlen

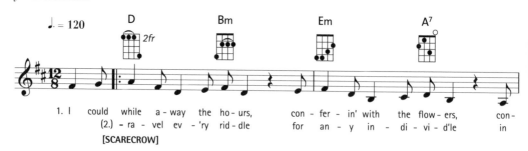

1. I could while a-way the ho-urs, con-fer-in' with the flow-ers, con-
(2.) -ra-vel ev-'ry rid-dle for an-y in-di-vi-d'le in
[SCARECROW]

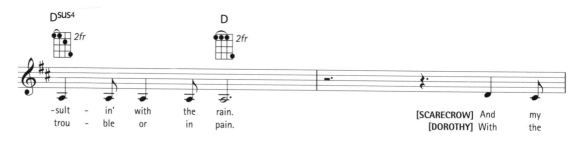

-sult- in' with the rain.
trou- ble or in pain.

[SCARECROW] And my
[DOROTHY] With the

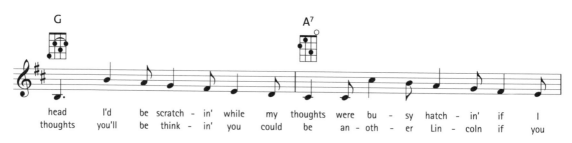

head I'd be scratch-in' while my thoughts were bu-sy hatch-in' if I
thoughts you'll be think-in' you could be an-oth-er Lin-coln if you

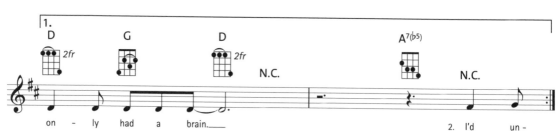

1.

N.C.

N.C.

on-ly had a brain.____

2. I'd un-

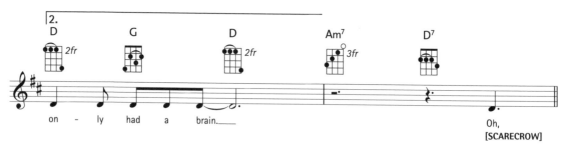

2.

on-ly had a brain.____

Oh,
[SCARECROW]

© Copyright 1939 EMI Feist Catalog Incorporated/EMI Catalogue Partnership.
EMI United Partnership Limited.
All Rights Reserved. International Copyright Secured.

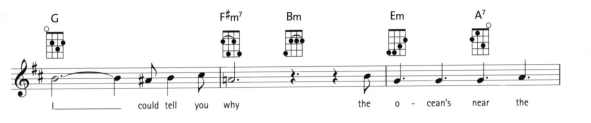

I_____ could tell you why the o - cean's near the

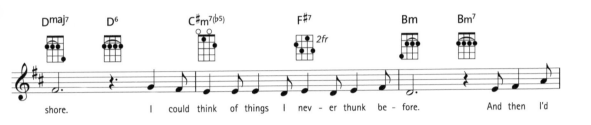

shore. I could think of things I nev – er thunk be – fore. And then I'd

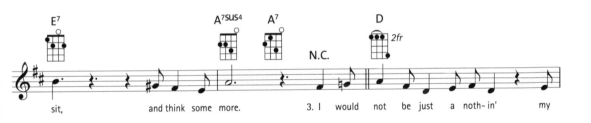

sit, and think some more. 3. I would not be just a noth- in' my

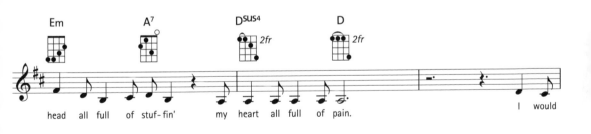

head all full of stuf- fin' my heart all full of pain. I would

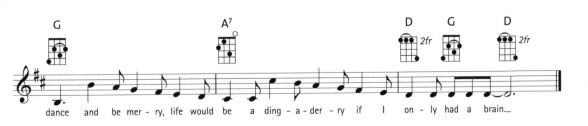

dance and be mer - ry, life would be a ding - a - der - ry if I on - ly had a brain.__

If I Only Had A Heart

Words by E.Y. Harburg
Music by Harold Arlen

© Copyright 1939 EMI Feist Catalog Incorporated/EMI Catalogue Partnership.
EMI United Partnership Limited.
All Rights Reserved. International Copyright Secured.

If I Only Had The Nerve

Words by E.Y. Harburg
Music by Harold Arlen

♩. = 110

[COWARDLY LION]

1. Yeah, it's sad, be-lieve me, mis-sy, when you're born to be a sis-sy with-
(2.) -fraid there's no de - ny - in': I'm just a dan - de - li - on, a

-out the vim and verve. But I
fate I don't de - serve. I'd be

could show my prow - ess, be a li - on, not a mou - ess if I
brave as a bliz - zard. [TIN MAN] I'd be gen - tle as a li - zard.

on - ly had the nerve.___ [SCARECROW] I'd be

2. I'm a - clev - er as a giz - zard. If the
[DOROTHY]

Wi - zard is a Wi - zard who will serve. Then I'm sure to get a
[SCARECROW]

© Copyright 1939 EMI Feist Catalog Incorporated/EMI Catalogue Partnership.
EMI United Partnership Limited.
All Rights Reserved. International Copyright Secured.

brain. A heart. A home. The nerve! Oh._____ We're

[TIN MAN] [DOROTHY] [COWARDLY LION] [ALL]

𝅗𝅥. = c. 130

off to see the Wi - zard,_____ the won - der - ful Wi - zard of Oz. We

hear he is a whiz of a wiz if ev - er a wiz there was. If ev - er, oh ev - er, a wiz there was, the

Wi - zard of Oz is one be - cause, be - cause, be - cause, be - cause, be - cause, be -

- cause,_____ be - cause of the won - der - ful things he does. We're

off to see the Wi - zard,_____ the won - der - ful Wi-zard of Oz!_____

Optimistic Voices
(You're Out Of The Woods)

Words by E.Y. Harburg
Music by Harold Arlen

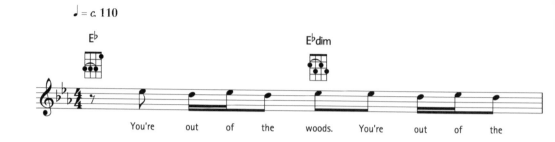

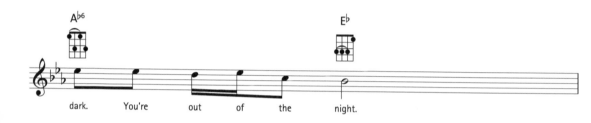

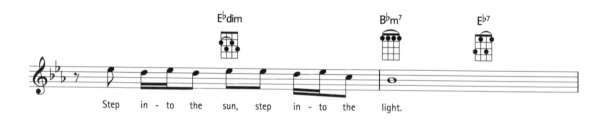

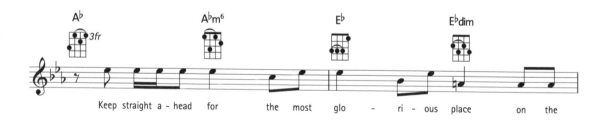

© Copyright 1939 EMI Feist Catalog Incorporated.
EMI United Partnership Limited.
All Rights Reserved. International Copyright Secured.

The Merry Old Land Of Oz

Words by E.Y. Harburg
Music by Harold Arlen

Ha, ha, ha, ho, ho, ho and a cou - ple of tra la las, that's

how we laugh the day a - way in the Mer - ry Old Land of Oz.

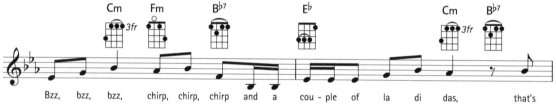

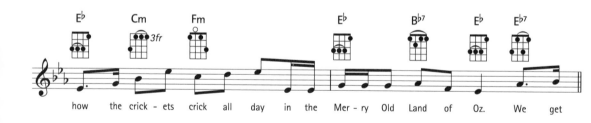

Bzz, bzz, bzz, chirp, chirp, chirp and a cou - ple of la di das, that's

how the crick - ets crick all day in the Mer - ry Old Land of Oz. We get

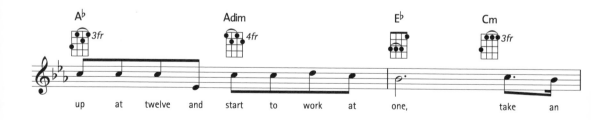

up at twelve and start to work at one, take an

© Copyright 1939 EMI Feist Catalog Incorporated.
EMI United Partnership Limited.
All Rights Reserved. International Copyright Secured.

hour for lunch and then at two we're done. Jol - ly good fun!

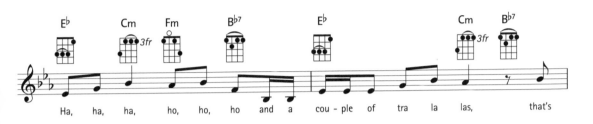

Ha, ha, ha, ho, ho, ho and a cou - ple of tra la las, that's

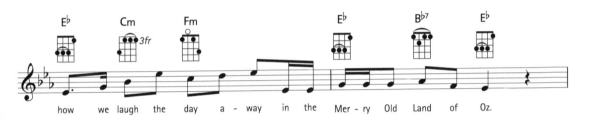

how we laugh the day a - way in the Mer - ry Old Land of Oz.

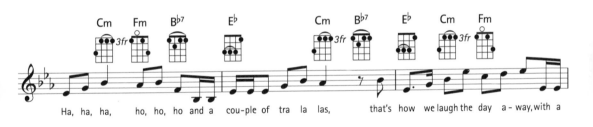

Ha, ha, ha, ho, ho, ho and a cou-ple of tra la las, that's how we laugh the day a - way, with a

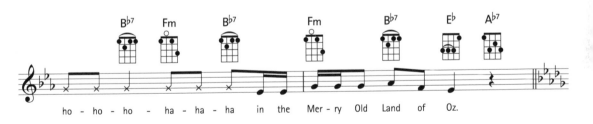

ho - ho - ho - ha - ha - ha in the Mer - ry Old Land of Oz.

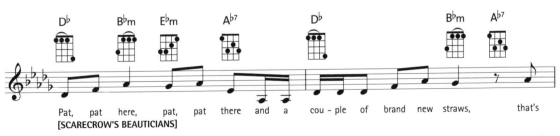

Pat, pat here, pat, pat there and a cou - ple of brand new straws, that's

[SCARECROW'S BEAUTICIANS]

31

how we keep you young and fair in the Mer-ry Old Land of Oz.

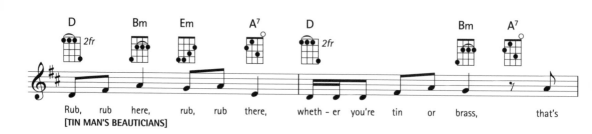

Rub, rub here, rub, rub there, wheth-er you're tin or brass, that's

[TIN MAN'S BEAUTICIANS]

how we keep you in re-pair in the Mer-ry Old Land of Oz. We can

[DOROTHY'S BEAUTICIANS]

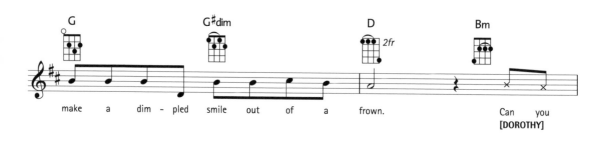

make a dim-pled smile out of a frown. Can you

[DOROTHY]

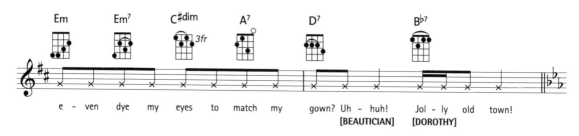

e-ven dye my eyes to match my gown? Uh-huh! Jol-ly old town!

[BEAUTICIAN]   [DOROTHY]

Clip, clip here, clip, clip there, we give the rough-est claws... That
[LION'S BEAUTICIANS]   [LION]

cer - tain air of sa - voir faire in the Mer-ry Old Land of Oz. Ha!

Ha, ha, ha... ho, ho, ho... ha, ha, ha, ha... ha! That's
[SCARECROW]   [TIN MAN]   [DOROTHY]   [LION]   [ALL]

how we laugh the day a - way in the Mer-ry Old Land of Oz. That's

how we laugh the day a - way, with a ho, ho, ho, ha, ha, ha, ha, ha, ha, ha, ha, ha,

ha, ha, ha, ha, ha, ha, in the Mer-ry Old Land of Oz.

If I Were The King Of The Forest

Words by E.Y. Harburg
Music by Harold Arlen

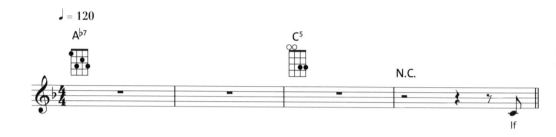

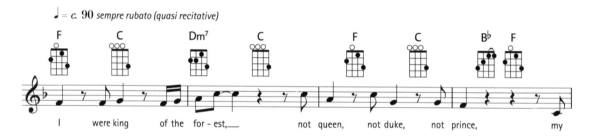

I were king of the for-est,___ not queen, not duke, not prince, my

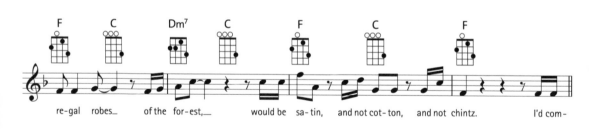

re-gal robes___ of the for-est,___ would be sa-tin, and not cot-ton, and not chintz. I'd com-

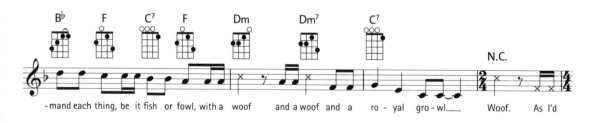

-mand each thing, be it fish or fowl, with a woof and a woof and a ro-yal gro-wl.___ Woof. As I'd

© Copyright 1939 EMI Feist Catalog Incorporated/EMI Catalogue Partnership.
EMI United Partnership Limited.
All Rights Reserved. International Copyright Secured.

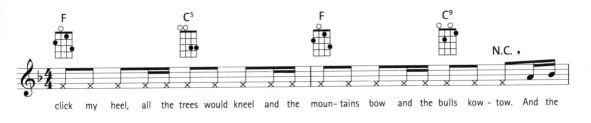

click my heel, all the trees would kneel and the moun-tains bow and the bulls kow-tow. And the

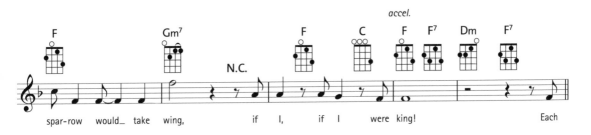

spar-row would_ take wing, if I, if I were king! Each

rab-bit would show re-spect to me. The chip-munks ge-nu-flect to me. Though my

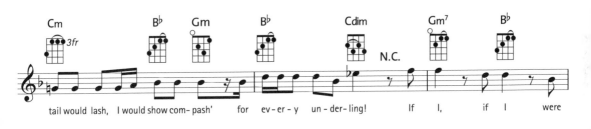

tail would lash, I would show com-pash' for ev-er-y un-der-ling! If I, if I were

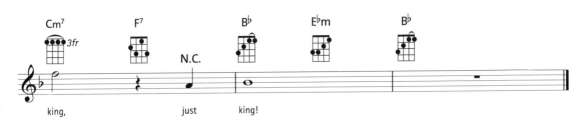

king, just king!

35

Over The Rainbow/
What A Wonderful World

Words by E.Y. Harburg
Music by Harold Arlen

Words & Music by Bob Thiele & George Weiss

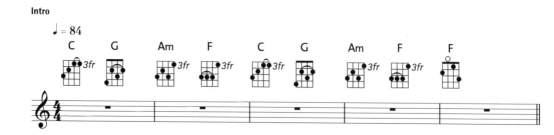

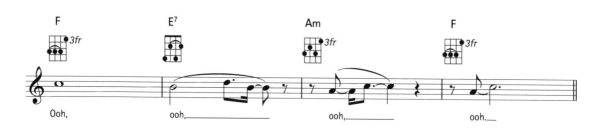

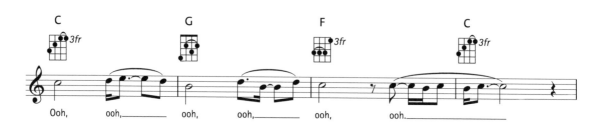

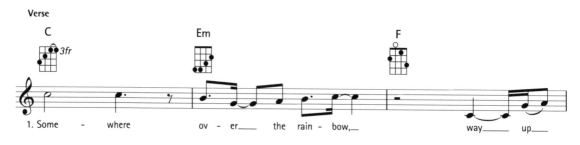

© Copyright 1939 EMI Feist Catalog Incorporated.
EMI United Partnership Limited.
All Rights Reserved. International Copyright Secured

© Copyright 1967 Abilene Music Inc./
Times Square Music Publications Company.
Carlin Music Corporation/Imagem Music.
All Rights Reserved. International Copyright Secured

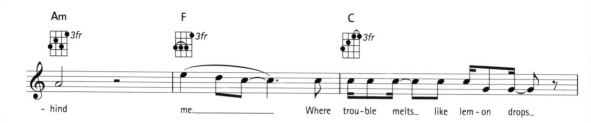

- hind me._____ Where trou-ble melts_ like lem-on drops_

high a-bove_ the chim - ney top that's_ where you'll find_____ me_____ oh.

Verse

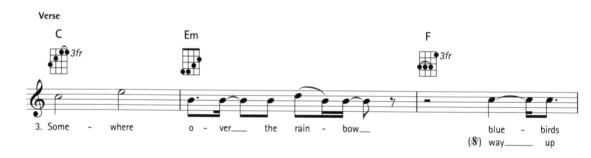

3. Some - where o - ver____ the rain - bow___ blue - birds
(𝄋) way_____ up

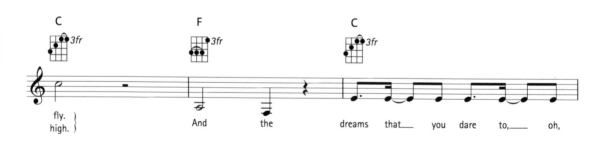

fly. }
high. }
And the dreams that___ you dare to,____ oh,

To Coda ⊕

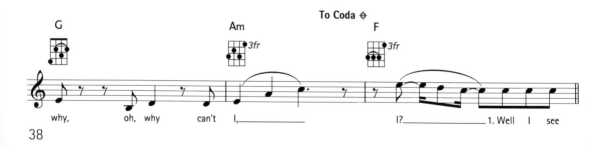

why, oh, why can't I,_____ I?_____ 1. Well I see

38

Verse

(1.) trees of green and___ red ros - es too. I'll watch them___ bloom for
(2.) skies of blue and I see clouds of white, and the bright - ness of day,

me and___ you. } And___ I think to my - self, what a won - der - ful
I like the dark. }

1.
world. 2. Well I see

2.
world. The

col - ors of the rain - bow, so pret - ty in the sky,___ are

al - so on the fac - es of peo - ple pass - ing by.___ I see friends shak - ing hands say - ing,

"How do you do?" They're real - ly say - ing, "I I___ love

39

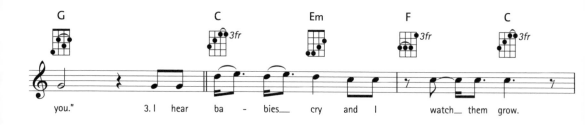
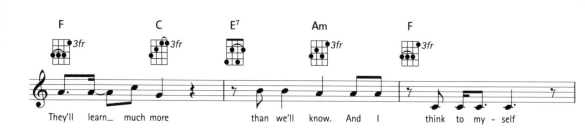
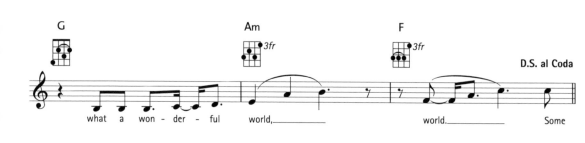
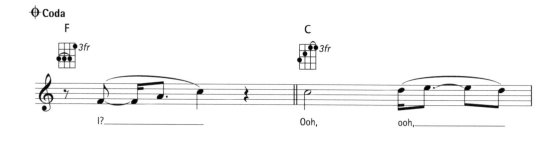
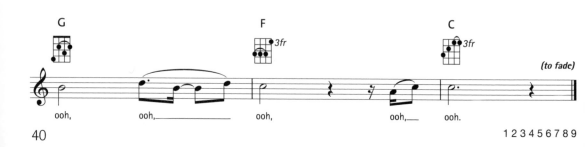

1 2 3 4 5 6 7 8 9